SONGS FOR COMING HOME

SONGS
· FOR ·
COMING
HOME

Poems by DAVID WHYTE

19 89

MANY RIVERS PRESS

LANGLEY, WASHINGTON

For my mother and father
and for all teachers, especially
Alec Barker, Derek Fry, *and* Bas Christie,
who shared the passionate hours
of discovery

Some of these poems have appeared in magazines,
newsletters and broadsheets, including *Resurgence, Seakayaker,*
and others.

Library of Congress Catalogue Card Number 88-92820

First published by Spring Valley Press 1984

Revised Edition.
COPYRIGHT © 1989 BY DAVID WHYTE

ISBN 0-9621524-0-4

. . . I cannot tell if the day
is ending, or the world, or if
the secret of secrets is inside me again.

—ANNA AKHMATOVA

Translated by Jane Kenyon

CONTENTS

CONTENTS [*continued*]

THE SONG OF THE LARK

The song begins and the eyes are lifted
but the sickle points toward the ground
its downward curve forgotten in the song she hears
while over the dark wood, rising or falling
the sun lifts on cool air
the small body of a singing lark.

The song falls, the eyes raise, the mouth opens
and her bare feet on the earth have stopped.

Whoever listens in this silence, as she listens
will also stand opened, thoughtless, frightened
by the joy she feels, the pathway in the field
branching to a hundred more, no one has explored.

What is called in her rises from the ground
and is found in her body,
what she is given is secret even from her.

This silence is the seed in her
of everything she is
and falling through her body
to the ground from which she comes
it finds a hidden place to grow
and rises, and flowers, in old wild places
where the dark-edged sickle cannot go.

[I]

SONGS FOR LEAVING THE HOUSE

ON THE RIM OF THE ISLAND

I WALK OUT from the house, taking my coat in anticipation
of the ruffling wind on the cliff. Sounds from the seashore
receive echoing correspondences inside my chest. One part
of my body reverberates with the springing grass, another
with the purple headland where I sense the waves are crashing.
At the turn in the road I feel the first fist of wind carrying
the shore smells, each smell distinguished by its own salty
ecstasy, felt like small hands moving in the stomach, each
gesture signaling a certain fragrance, each movement like a
slight lift of air in the belly settles out into something larger,
radiating out through the arms. I reach the cliff which is
the rim of the island and the power undergirding the water
rises against it, fueling the swelling configurations of the body
and sounding a deep bass note on the underbelly of the rock.
Now there are only individual sounds threaded together by
the same hands that earlier moved in the stomach, each
giving momentum to the next and seeming to turn the whole
body like a huge wheel. The edge of the cliff is very fragile
and I am careful not to walk too near. This delicacy surround-
ing me makes me move slowly, each step cushioned from
the earth by thick grass. Moving like this the skin prickles
and undulates in the wind and the updraft lifts the palms
out from the body, as on the rim of the island
I begin to dance.

ALONE IN THE FOREST

It is only in the forest that I realize how many rooted structures exist inside of me, and it is in the forest now, with my breath lifting in billowing spirals in the cold air, that I am suddenly released into the miracle of small things; — a bird's movement on a branch, the sound of water still dripping from yesterday's rainstorm. In the forest everything in the mind can be given away, so that the heart can be open to the intense concentration that natural objects demand. Through this concentration where nothing exists but the object itself, enormous energy opens out through the woodland silhouette. By allowing this silence, nothing is held in the mind beyond the time in which it happens: the undergrowth rustles without judgment, the marsh can sleep undisturbed by comparison or memory. Out of this emerges an energy that can only be described as *praise*; and as this intensifies, even this must give way like the distant call in the forest, so that this energy opens up a void in the center of all things. At this point the praise suddenly becomes mutual and I stand revealed . . . and even this in no way diminishes this luxuriant moss-covered log which creaks, scattering the birds as I sit on it.

COMING BACK TO THE HOUSE

COMING BACK TO THE HOUSE, I lean down into the snow and pick it up with both hands, where it shivers like a small animal stirred by the cold breeze: — a black leaf, torn in the center, a swirly criss-cross of dark and striated white put there with startling urgency. One gaping hole shows me how a cut edge crinkles. There is a small curve at one end where a piece of grass sticks to it. In my closing hands it makes a sound like parchment, but nothing is written. It is cut, torn and fragile, and balances on only a thin line of its stem . . . a fallen leaf three months after even the last of summer, how dark it seems against the snow! Entering the house I walk over to the table and put it down, and touching one end I make the leaf rock. A cradle for quiet thoughts as night draws close.

[II]

SONGS FOR THE MOMENTS

HORSES MOVING ON THE SNOW

In winter
through the damp grass
around the house
there are horses moving
on the snow

in the half-light
they move quickly

following the fence
until the mist takes them
    completely

and evening
is the hollow sound of hooves
in the south field.

SOUND OVER WATER

Small spots of rain hiss in the fire
twigs crack in the hot coals
out in the lake
the bright dash of trout
then silence.

From darkness
an oar dips on the still surface
stirring silence
as the first shadow of a boat draws near.

The ancient trunks gather invisibly
from the fire
smoke swirls like liquid stirred in a chalice

The boat touches shore
sounding on gravel

And distant parts of the night
leap in the fire.

LIGHT OVER WATER

Through the light on the upper line of water
three birds
with wings extended into the center of brightness
turn south into the channel
flicking their wings through the currents of air
to a silent horizon that empties the wind of sound.

In that noiseless wind they turn
and in the sudden gusts as they lift
the dark throats of the evening birds turn white.

THE GEESE

Brightness and black specks
lift from the water

and from the geese
sound breaks over the lake
of wings beating through a clear sun.

Their necks extend upward
to the rim of the white mountain
where they close
tightening
northward
into the black line of an arrow.

Each morning the old one rises
strings his bow
aims in the clear sun
and breaking the silence
with beating wings
looses the geese from bent arms.

LEAVING THE GATE

As I leave the gate
the alder
black-leaded in a rising sky
is still.

On the pathway's gravel
pierced black with stones
my foot cracks on a dry leaf.

The eyes search
the path remains
the small stones crowding
still piercing
the dry leaf lets go of sound
and lets a crow cry darkness from the ridge.

Evening gathers
the gate closes
I wait
the latch clicks
and I leave the gate.

[III]

SONGS FOR THE BODY

INSIDE

Inside this sitting here: —
this mind pulling knees up
     close to the chest
     with tense hands.

Inside this
movement of anxiety for the body
and its worries of money
and its teeth grinning falsely
to the solution of all things surrounding

is the seed
and the hands pressing down into the soil
and the dreams of generation
in the seed about to wake.

Tonight I will sleep with my worries
through dreams dark with soil
and the heaving cataclysm of the spade
turning earth round me
not speaking of air
or light fused with greenness
but of darkness
and the first leaves
like hands in prayer
clasped inside the seed.

UP ON THE HILL'S BACK

Up on the hill's back
field lines have stopped
memories still pass the next horizon
nothing halts the age of the body walking
not the young growth of trees
nor the fallen trunk across the hill path.

When I have passed this way
the crows
will still bear down fiercely from the west
the lights wink on
and night come bringing rain
sweeping the branches down

life passes
and clouds mound darkness in the west
where the path turns
grass breaks in furrows down the hill

whoever asks of darkness
must touch the darkness in himself
whoever asks of grass
bend down in the moving stalks
and under the blades
feel the small birds shivering
waiting to rise in the morning light.

ALL MY BODY CALLS

All my body calls
for something in this sleeping
earth
we call the spirit.

But how
from lifted arms
where stars run through fingers
and the night is like sand
do I breathe a fragrance of its wisdom
do I call its name
or listen to the drops
that trickle down to earth
and hear
life being given
not only through the moving hands of the forest
but through the hand that reaches in
the dark unmoving regions of the chest
and uncovers slowly
the enormous
indistinct
shape of the ocean.

BODY OF OCEANS

FOR MY GRANDFATHER, WHO DIED
IN A HOSPITAL WARD

Body immobile
body of oceans
confluence of arms and legs
whose arteries have met all these years
in the city and shorefronts
of muscle and sinew
do not go
where the sun tortures by day
and the night no longer
whispers its eternal things.

Body resisted
body unmoved
by suffering, in the heart
there are the chambers of the heart
and in the chambers there is the gentle
folding of memories
as the pulse falls and life
is packed in the hallways:
at the door
there are the entrails
coiling to the dreams of remembered meals
and the pressures of release
in liquid earth
add urgency to the hands folding memories
as the waters draw near.

Body unfolded
body of flowers
in the seeming cruelty
of the angel of urine and life
there are the tunnels of secretion
and the petals falling
through the hand uplifted in the stomach
and the grief
of the body falling
becomes water as the sky turns dark

lightly now
the rain is falling on the fields
into silence.

THE LONG ARM OF MEMORY

The long arm of memory
winds round the frozen shoulder
I lean against a wall
calling me back
as if I could
go
from this place.

Often I have unwound that arm
and flown above the town
where I and all my friends have slept
night upon night
uncurled it like the wing a moth
could show to a new world
born to its hundred changing eyes
to the veins of its body
to the fur that stretches down its chest
to its leap in a world gone mad with flight.

[IV]

SONGS FOR PRAISE

THE OPENING OF EYES *After R. S. Thomas*

That day I saw beneath dark clouds
the passing light over the water
and I heard the voice of the world speak out,
I knew then, as I had before
life is no passing memory of what has been
nor the remaining pages in a great book
waiting to be read.

It is the opening of eyes long closed.
It is the vision of far off things
seen for the silence they hold.
It is the heart after years
of secret conversing
speaking out loud in the clear air.

It is Moses in the desert
fallen to his knees before the lit bush.
It is the man throwing away his shoes
as if to enter heaven
and finding himself astonished,
opened at last,
fallen in love with solid ground.

TREES

In writing about trees
the hand
should burst a thousand leaves
on the page
or spread in silhouette
the curled branches
between words

so that as we read
the white hollows between words
can be the wind
or in certain poems, stillness
so that as eyes
descend the page, smoke rises
straight
toward heaven

as the lines descend down
to the roots
the page is straining
so that the lower square of paper
seethes with immensity
unable to be moved, only tugged
or hurled massively over
when the page turns

when the hand does touch
the paper
the feeling of age
is immediate
the feel of wood
grains the forehead
or curves the back
like mountain ash
tenacious
between stones

by the last line
we sink our weight
through dreams of earth
holding the ground for a hundred
years of time
unable to forget
a promise with the land
to breathe
and with our arms
hold heaven close to earth.

GRASS

Grass breaking out
through the knees

legs kneeling
on grass in the cities
on a porcupine of green spears
between vacant lots

grass through the temples

even here, luminous
through old cans
the Buddha with
a beard of green moss

grass across the landing strips

through the hollow wind
of glass and steel
burning the tongues of infants

grass on the lips of the watcher

at midnight
black grass
and broken glass
on bare feet

clumps of soil trenched
with roots
and sods
breaking cement

spreading seeds across the freeway

intensity from the sun
shape from the air
passion of the earth
grass.

THE WILDFLOWER

In the center of this wildflower
the names of things revolve like planets
and as if pulled by tides
and the gravity of deep space
the names of things move into form
through enormous distance.

Like electrons enchanted
by the atom
they show their undiscovered seas
as they revolve.

But for this dark flower
I give it the name of a hidden moon.

[V]

SONGS WITHOUT WISDOM

TODAY I HAVE NO WISDOM

I have walked blessed and bareheaded
on the seashore
with as little wisdom as the opened clam
its dead mouth streaming with sand
or the birds half sunk
in shallow halls of wood-trunk and tide pool.

I have listened with the small acuity of
crabshell on rock
of water falling through sand
of the tide coming home
to a welcome on by boot-tops
and always
moving everywhere
the sea air is running hands over my open neck.

I have never learned to tread quietly here
where sounds are always rushing on the beach
or upward with the gulls,
on an open beach
a voice can be tenacious in the wind
and the chest heaves to snatch a breath
and cry again.

For today I have no wisdom but that of sand
heaving from some dream that sleeps beneath the tide
until I come with my voice bellowing
and my small child's heart
and I walk through the sea-spume
like a man walking through sparks
or an intense fire where the heart ignites
and explodes leaving nothing
not an ember of wisdom to warm me

It is all consumed in the moment
the dazzling
upward

flame of pure presence.

THE CLIFF

Wind explodes on the cliff
and the voice is still heard
from the water
moaning
low and rumored
like the brass belly of a hunting horn

and the arms open to take its breath
and hear it shouting
of the urgent sea on the rocks below
of the hands gathering sand
and of the air
combing the wild feathers of a single gull

there is a fierceness here
that takes the shoulders of the soul
and shakes it
into whiteness, into the falling horse-tails
of succeeding waves
where it laughs, undaunted, broken open
into its own hugeness
into the thunder that goes beyond the sea
and lifts

and rises as the wave recedes.

UNDER THE LOCUST TREES

Under the locust trees
the body is tired
and the arms
are streaked with shadows
and the mind begins to arrange
and place the light
and catalogue the smells
and rolling slightly
on the undulations of the lawn
feel the hard
and the soft
and recognize the smell
penetrating the skin
of sun-warmed bark.

A bird calls
and the sound
falls into the clearing
like a single drop
pushing everything to the brim
and spills over
flowing
through the thick currents of air
above the grass

winding under the trees
beneath the sun
until
snaking
as something cool and green
outside the mind

we slip through the afternoon
currents
green with clover
where we shed our skins
and coil again
fallen to sleep in the summer sun.

[VI]

SONGS FROM THE KAYAK

I

The kayak
slips through a delicate channel
between islands

this slight shape
cutting deep green

for ten thousand years
the skin of
northern seals
nosing between ice floes

now the russet glow
of orange fiberglass
translucent

floating at the edge
of evening

until dark comes
and the paddle reaches
in the deep night
and dips between the Pleiades

silently now
the kayak
nudges between stars.

II

This freedom
as the kayak nuzzles through kelp!

In the sea
for each paddle stirring the waters
there are the tones of color
and for the lifting bow
there is the horizon
and shades of purple
in the islands to the west
and the short slapping waves
splash colors
as the thin skin
leaps forward

moving
intently
a sense of journey
through kelp
spread low on the ocean rim.

III

Balanced in the water
this cradle of new journeys
the kayak
allows me to fish
peering down
to other worlds
where creatures breathe
the dark water

I lean over in the warm night

and rock on the sleeping chest
of the Georgia Strait
careful not to go too far
and wake the giant
whose limbs stretch liquid
in the full moon
reflecting from fiords
onto steep cliffs

no journeys tonight
no wisdom
one place with a rod and line
and the fish will leap in my net!

IV

From the northeast
undercurrents stirred by wind
ripple south
under the kayak
and with each rise
the boat lifts
to the dark clouds
covering Spieden

with hips awash
and bow submerged
each stroke
balanced on unseen pressures
lives for a moment
in the shoulders

and with the first sound
of indrawn breath
the heart begins to flow
and become liquid
spinning through the arms
like molten glass

out here
life is a vibrant wire
pulled tight
between two opposing limbs

and it sings to the touch of the ocean.

V

The kayak is no place for brooding on the world!
one star slips by
a paddle stirs in the silver light.

VI

When the mind lets go at last
the kayak can roll with the waves
following those green hillsides
to the very bottom.

And in each wave
pierced by the bow
the rattling sound of raven bones
breaks into flowers
falling to the southeast.

In my arms
shapes enter from the air
darken like the wings of a bird
then leave in the water.

In my voice
I hear the old one waking at last
calling the ravens
with spume-filled wings
in and out of the chest.

His body is hardened by cold,
when the sun breaks through
salt
sparkles from his back.

His hands have crushed
and thrown across the water
the ashes of his campfires
so that each place he leaves
floats out before him
and everywhere
he finds the places he has left
renewed like the ashes
lifted and scattered in the wind.

Even here
paddling the purple line
where inland water meets ocean
and light sweeps the mind clean
we find a place to be together
— old friends after long parting —
a final campfire
as the sun goes down.

Others look to find us
what do they see?

Two white stumps
bleached by the sun
where the waves come in.

OUT ON THE OCEAN

In these waves
I am caught on shoulders
lifting the sky

each crest
breaks sharply
and suddenly rises

in each steep wall
my arms work in the strong movement
of other arms

the immense energy
each wave throws up with hand outstretched
grabs the paddle

the blades flash
lifting veils of spray as the bow rears
terrified then falls

with five miles to go
of open ocean
the eyes pierce the horizon

the kayak pulls round
like a pony held by unseen reins
shying out of the ocean

and the spark behind fear
recognized as life
leaps into flame

★

always this energy smoulders inside
when it remains unlit
the body fills with dense smoke.

[VII]

SONGS FOR COMING HOME

HOME

Home:
A long road on the raven coast
on the roof
two kayaks
bend through the warm air
a resonant hum
in their tight ropes
sings in the evening light.

Headlights switched on
as the car dips through hollows
and the colors deepen.

We all speak together
or are silent.

At Deception Pass
the water ripples
under our bellies
and our souls leap
in a sudden feeling
to swim north
with salmon eyes
nudging between islands.

The western sky warms
and we ease through the land

two lights
in the slowly moving darkness

outside
dew gathers on dry branches

my wife turns
speaks to me
reminds me of a crossing
yesterday
on a calm sea
and we laugh in the dark interior
of the car

with two friends fallen asleep
in the back
heading south through the
dark night
and home.

SEVEN STEPS FOR COMING HOME

Oh pure contradiction . . . Rilke

One step to take notice
the next one to look and to praise
the third *to be* praised
the fourth is strangely for love
the fifth is to be
caught between water and sky.

The sixth is return
the seventh unspeakable
except in
one small stolen poem
flawed by the heart
spoken to one other
in secret
never to be said again.

After this look down at the paper
and see who is writing.
Your hands! Only your hands!

A pure contradiction,
a pure blessing.
Everything you learned
has come to nothing.

Other books by David Whyte

WHERE MANY RIVERS MEET